PRESS INTERVIEW FUNDAMENTALS

TECHNIQUES FOR MASTERING INTERVIEWS

By Lynn F. Austin

Copyright © 2016 Austin Group Consulting
All rights reserved.

ISBN:
978-0-9973227-1-2
978-0-9973227-2-9

This book is dedicated to my family, friends and clients.

Table of Contents

1. Style and Substance

2. Effective Press Interviews

3. Things To Consider

4. Crafting the Message

5. The Interview

6. Getting Back to Message

7. Putting Words in Your Mouth

Introduction

Let me take a moment to say thank you for purchasing this book designed to provide you with the fundamentals of press and media interviewing.
This guide will properly prepare you for interviews with electronic, digital and print media.

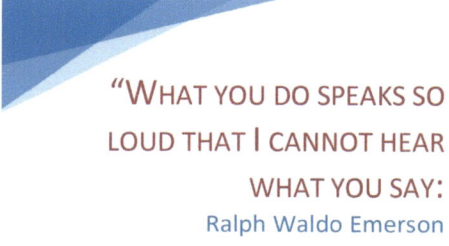

"What you do speaks so loud that I cannot hear what you say:
Ralph Waldo Emerson

I realize there are many other resources out there competing for your attention, and I appreciate you entrusting me to help you achieve your goals.

When it comes to the interview, there are two basic components of a "good" interview are 1) style – how you look; and 2) substance – what you say.

The inspiration behind this book is to help people understand that Style and Substance can determine how well what you say is actually accepted and absorbed by an audience.

In this book, you'll get information in key areas the interview including **Style and Substance; Things To Consider; Crafting the Message; The Interview Presentation; Getting Back to Message and Putting Words in Your Mouth.** Interviews can be what you need and want them to be and I'll show you how.

Acknowledgements

Thank you to my supporters, mentors and coaches. This book would not have been possible without the tireless encouragement of my community of accountabilities partners from the Ultimate Success Masterclass.

I would also like to thank my visionary and break through leadership coach, Natalie Ledwell of the Mind Movies community for helping me understand that I have everything inside me to succeed.

About The Author

Lynn is managing director at Austin Group Consulting, LLC, a brand, public relations and executive leadership development firm designed to coach, guide and empower transformational visionary leadership development.

With more than 15 years of executive lead-ership experience at fortune 500 companies, Lynn's professional portfolio include lead-ership roles at Aston Martin, Jaguar, Land Rover and Harley-Davidson Motor Compa-ny. Lynn graduated Magna Cum Laude from Washington Adventist University, earned an MBA from Capella University. She holds a Six Sigma Green Belt Certification and is both an Ultimate

Success Masterclass graduate and Coach

Lynn Austin, is someone with first-hand knowledge and experience as both the interviewer as well as the interviewee. When it comes to press inter-views, it helps to have the tips and techniques on realities of the press inter-view. With a good foundation and understanding of the process—walking in to an interview, you can make the experience one filled with all you hoped to accomplish.

Interviews give you the opportunity to put out a message to the world and this guide will show you how to have a smart, business-savvy approach to an effective interview experience.

Chapter One

Style and Substance

PRESS INTERVIEW FUNDAMENTALS

STYLE

Eye contact
- Look at your interviewer and only your interviewer when you are talking
- If the interview is remote-style, look at the camera lens.

Positioning
- Men – Put both feet on the floor without crossing your legs
- Women – It is acceptable to cross legs at either the knee or ankles

Hands
- Use your hands naturally, hand gestures help you to be a "real person" for your audience

Live TV
- Be yourself, at your best and tell what you want to tell.

Clothing
- In general conservative is best – no checks, stripes or busy patterns that will distract your audience from what you are saying.
  - Men: Solid blue/gray suits; blue or pastel (not white) shirt and non-flashy bold-patterned tie.
  - Women – Strong colors (preferably not black or red); skirts should cover knees; makeup should be subtle; avoid dangling earrings or flashy jewelry

At the end, remain seated until told you're off the air!

 **Press Interview Fundamentals**

Substance

Preparation
- Be prepared – you **MUST** know your subject matter thoroughly to be able to communicate effectively.
- Limit yourself to three principal or key messages.
- Bridge –Acknowledge the question then deliver your own positive message (reference transitional phrases).
- If applicable, try to use a catchy, memorable phrase that is easily repeatable. Keep it short and simple.
- Don't ramble with your message, you will lose your audience and your credibility on the subject.
- To ensure you deliver your message, try starting with your conclusion or the main point you want to make, then build on it with your three key points.
- Be truthful and straightforward.
- If you don't know an answer it's ok to respond saying that the question is not your area of expertise, or simply state "I don't know the answer to that, but what I do know is" and transition back to your main points.
- If you disagree with the question or the question contains inaccurate information that you disagree with, challenge it firmly but politely. This is particularly important with print interviews.
- Don't use a lot of jargon, slang, technical language or acronyms that your audience may not understand.
- Look at every question as an opportunity to make your three points.
- With telephone or radio interviews, make sure your voice sounds energized to help you communicate since you don't have eye contact.
- Tell your story, enjoy the experience and remember, your goal is to deliver and control content being reported

Remember, the interviewer is NOT your friend, nor is he/she your enemy and remember NOTHING is off the record.

If you don't want to see it in print, social media or hear on the air, DO NOT say it to the reporter.

Chapter Two

Effective Press Interviews

PRESS INTERVIEW FUNDAMENTALS

EFFECTIVE PRESS INTERVIEWS

Reporters are in the business of telling stories that people want to read, hear and watch. The "interesting" always manages to crowd out the important as we'll discuss later with critical considerations.

> "The only thing I have wanted to do in my life—and the only thing I have done somewhat well—is telling stories… For me, stories are like toys, and making them up is, one way or another, like a game. I believe that if a child were put in front of a group of toys with different characteristics, this child would start by playing with everything but at the end would stick to only one of those toys. This one toy would be the expression of the kid's skills and vocation…
>
> If conditions were given for this talent to be developed throughout a lifetime, we would be on the verge of discovering one of the secrets for happiness and longevity."
>
> —*Gabriel García Márquez*

Let's glance at Journalism and Journalists

A Breakdown of Journalism
- For the most part, the behavior of reporters is predicable
- To an outsider, behavior may seem somewhat petty, arbitrary or vicious
    - Trust and know that there is almost always an "interesting" agenda

Journalists
- Reporters as a group behave in predictable ways
- Predicting behavior it important to know their;
    - Value systems
    - Decision-making mechanisms
    - Social relationships within the group
    - Social and power relationships within the group and among other journalists
    - Behavioral triggers

Effective Press Interviews

Understanding / Misunderstanding Journalists
- Thinking journalists focus on what's important
- Thinking journalists' first amendment role places some type of responsibility upon them
- Thinking that journalists' core values-- fairness, accuracy and balance—mean the same thing as when a non- journalist uses them.

- Journalist are in the business of telling stories people want to read or watch
- Given a choice between the important and the interesting, journalists will choose interesting every time for example:
  - More reporters gathered in front of the NY Federal Courthouse for Martha Stewart's trial than for any prior event, including World Trade Center bombing verdicts
  - There were five times as many journalists covering the verdict at the Michael Jackson trial than were accredited to the war in Iraq.

Chapter Three

Things To Consider

Things To Consider

In general, most interviews are con-ducted to report on one of five areas: conflict, contradiction, controversy, colorful language, cast of characters. Understanding these considerations helps you best prepare for the press interview, give consideration to "why" you are to be interviewed, and/or to respectfully decline the interview if necessary.

Following is a detailed breakdown of each area to enlightened you and help you understand what may be behind the interviewer's intent:

Conflict
- The slightest hint of conflict becomes the central element of the story, out of all proportion to the rest of the story
- The higher up in an organization, the better

Why?
- We identify conflict as a central narrative device
- It's easy to write and read conflict stories – which is why political reporters focus on who's ahead/behind – rather than on policy.

Things To Consider
Continued

Contradiction
- While conflict is more intriguing, contradiction is actually more common
- Conflict generally involves disputes between two people or entities, while contradiction can be caused by language.
- Contradiction is the most common narrative device used by journalists

Frequency of Contradiction
- Nearly every front page story begins with some type of contradiction.

Types of Contradiction
- Against conventional wisdom: "you might think this, but really not this
- Role reversal
- Reversal of fortune
- Saying the opposite of what you previously said
- Behaving different from how you said you would
- Violating values
- Changing your mind
- Juxtaposition of contrary ideas
- Mixing categories (size, temperature
- Using words with multiple meanings
- Irony
- Paradox
- Oxymoron

Things To Consider
CONTINUED

Controversy
- A topic already newsworthy
- A controversial topic that plays into a contradiction the further plays into a conflict

Colorful Language
- Colorful language is quotable language
    - Short
    - Vivid
    - Active Voice
    - Clear
    - Interesting

Cast of Characters
- An interview is not a conversation, deposition, or about the questions.
- An interview is a presentation that's only occasionally interrupted by questions.

With any request for an interview, each should be taken into account as you prepare for the interview or chose to decline.

Chapter Four

Crafting the Message

Crafting The Message

Your message is an essential component of your interview and becomes your reason for the interview. In crafting the message, consider the following:

1. What is the most important thought you want the audience to know, understand, internalize?
2. What is the second most important?
3. What is the third most important?

The three "most important" thoughts or ideas you want to convey are essentially the outline of your interview "presentation."

Chapter Five

The Interview

The Interview Presentation

In preparing for your interview, consider what you want to discuss – what thoughts, ideas, programs, products etc. you need to share with your audience.

1. Stress that you will discuss three (3) things.
2. Summarize and number each
   - First
   - Second
   - Third
3. Elaborate on each
   - First…
   - Second…
   - Third

While this may seem tedious, it is very important to your ability to understand your message, articulate your message and stay on point with your message during the interview.

Chapter Six

Getting Back to Message

Getting Back To Message

Because you have prepared and studied your key points, you both know and understand your message. This will help you stay on point, but also get back to your message as you are being asked questions

1. Acknowledge
    - Answer
    - Decline to answer
    - Recast
2. Transition
    - And…
    - But…
    - Linking word or phrase
    - Chain of reasoning
3. Back to the Message and Elaborate

Using this approach will help to ensure you are able to communicate your message and/or transition back to your message if necessary.

Chapter Seven

Putting Words in Your Mouth

Putting Words In Your Mouth

If you allow them to, reporters will try to "put words in your mouth" if for no other reason than to create one of the critical considerations discussed earlier. Here are some tips on how to address several notable realities during the interview and not allow reporters to put words into your mouth.

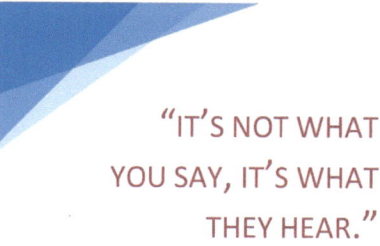

"IT'S NOT WHAT YOU SAY, IT'S WHAT THEY HEAR."

If you are asked, faced with or given:

A **Forced** Choice: Reject it and return to your three points

A **Hypothetical**: Don't speculate and transition back to your three points

Paraphrase: Don't allow the reporter to paraphrase your message, transition back and restate your message

Mistake: Correct the mistake and transition back to your message

Inflammatory Word: Don't repeat it.

PRESS INTERVIEW FUNDAMENTALS

TRANSITIONAL PHRASES
PHRASES TO HELP YOU GET YOUR POINT ACROSS OR BACK ON MESSAGE

- But the point I'd like to make is…
- The real point is…
- Let me add something to that…
- Another thing I'd like to mention…
- Let me mention something else…
- There's something else I'd like to point out…
- Another Point I'd like to make…
- There's another aspect to that question I'd like the viewer to focus on…
- There's something else we should be looking at…
- On a related topic, let me say…
- That's not really the issue; the issue is…
- That's not the question, the question is…
- The questions I get asked most often is…
- Let me answer this way…
- I think the best way to answer that is to tell you what we're trying to do…
- If you're asking me (phrase in your own terms)…
- Before I answer that, let me point out that…
- First, let me point out if I may…

Responses to contentious questions

- I think you have to look at it from a different perspective…
- That's not the way we see it at (name your company)
- There's another way to look at that…
- Are you saying…? What I'm saying is… (then state what you want)

Use with caution
- (Reporters Name) that's not the question I was hoping you'd ask

Press Interview Fundamentals

Media / Press Interview Template

1) Indicate discuss 3 things; 2) Summarize / Enumerate each; 3) Elaborate on each

There are three things I'd like to focus on…
Message 1:_____

Message 2:_____

Message 3:_____

Let me tell you more about my first point…
Support point_____

Support point_____

Support point_____

Let me tell you more about my second point…
Support point_____

Support point_____

Support point_____

Let me tell you more about my third point…
Support point_____

Support point_____

Support point_____

©2016 Austin Group Consulting,LLC

Conclusion

So there we have it – now, you can look at a press interview in a whole new light. We've picked out some of the most important details of what discuss, how to communicate your message, and how to make sure you leave your audience with the messages you intended to leave them with. In this book we have provided insight on:

- How to outline your interview
- Crafting your message to ensure you know and say what you mean to say
- Handling yourself in situations where you need to transition or get back to your message.
- Making the most of issues and scenarios within the interview.

While every interviewer is different you can greatly improve your success with interviews and in making a lasting impact on your audience.

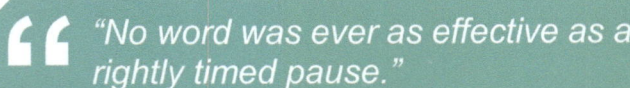

> "No word was ever as effective as a rightly timed pause."
>
> Mark Twain.

PRESS INTERVIEW FUNDAMENTALS

For more information on dealing with the new media or to schedule press interview fundamentals training

Contact us at:
www.austingroupconsulting.com

www.ingramcontent.com/pod-product-compliance
Lightning Source LLC
Chambersburg PA
CBHW041756040426
42446CB00001B/51